THE SERMONIC VERSES
100 SONNETS
ON LIFE, LIVING, LOVE & DEATH

N P SAMAL

BlueRose
Publishers
NewDelhi • London

First Published in January 2022

ISBN: 978-93-5472-813-6

BLUEROSE PUBLISHERS
www.bluerosepublishers.com
info@bluerosepublishers.com
+91 8882 898 898

Cover Design:
Aveek

Typographic Design:
Rohit

Distributed by: BlueRose, Amazon, Flipkart

ACKNOWLEDGEMENTS

With my deepest gratitude and thankfulness, I feel excited to acknowledge the following persons for their instrumental contributions without whom this book would not have been possible.

Dr. G.C. Nayak, the Chairman, MIET Group of Institutions, Odisha, who I am deeply indebted to for his priceless support and encouragement.

Prof. S.K. Joshi, the former Head, Department of English, Ravenshaw University, Odisha, for his continuous guidance and mentorship.

Prof. Dr. Sachidananda Panda, BPUT, Odisha, for his contribution of Foreword for this book as well as his significant assistance in editing.

Prof. Dr. G.K. Das, Principal, IGIPS, Bhubaneswar, for facilitating my work during the college hours.

Mr. Jyoti Ranjan Sahoo who is my technical advisor and promoter of philosophical and intellectual perspectives in me.

My daughter, Rashmirekha(Mama), who is the principal source of my inspiration and Mrs. Jayashree Beura, my wife, for putting up with me throughout my arduous occupation in writing this book.

My childhood friends, Mr. Sanjay Kumar Rath, Asst. Commissioner, EPFO, Odisha, and Mr. Arabinda Rath, Sr. Advocate, Odisha High Court, for their life-long intellectual inputs.

To
My daughter
MAMA
Of whom
This book is an incarnation.

Dear Mama,

I had been childless till I was fifty when you graced my life. Though you made your sojourn as brief as a few months, this divine gift of fatherhood has become a windfall for me to create an epoch. My life, barren as desert, metamorphosed into woodland with your monsoonal ingress, and has turned evergreen with the never-ending fragrance of verses of humanity. This is in your memory, I keep my journey to eternity.

With soulful love for you
Your father
N P Samal

FOREWORD

This would be an honest admission to acknowledge that I was caught unwarranted and literally surprised when

Prof N. P. Samal requested me to write the Foreword for his second volume of hundred sonnets. Mr. Samal is one amongst my few close acquaintances in the entire fraternity; those are passionate about literature and poetry in particular. In this current crisis, when the covid-19 pandemic is on the rampage when life is stuck at squire one, and confinement and human contact has become taboo, while being within the approved limitations, Mr. Samal's effort to reach out to the society at large, through his creative pursuit is highly commendable.

When free verse has become the go of society, a touch of vintage flavor becomes a show stopper. Mr. Samal is one amongst few poets of recent times, who keep abreast that fine fragrance of 'sonnets' to give wings to their inner emotions. It is quite engaging to go through his sonnets and the metrical dexterity he has mastered. I had been a regular visitor of his web page https://mypoems.npsamal.com, and have been fascinated by a variety of poems in free verse, as well as in rhyming forms often at other digital platforms too. His themes encompass a wide array of romantic, socio-political, cultural and philosophical subjects. The most striking thing about his poems is his fine balance between the contemporary and the conventional expressions, besides his experiments with different forms.

It is a mission, a vow, and I should call it a sort of madness in him, to give it back to the society he owes a lot, by touching others' lives, expanding the circle of our concern to include others, being authentic, and being always open to receive suggestions and inputs, so as to encompass the bulk of the finer aspects and angles of life unattended yet through his verses. This is no fairy tale, rather an honest description of many of the most amazing people I've encountered in my life and Mr. Samal fits into it by his own rights. This book captures that philosophy and shows that it is more than just a collection of some of his exceptional verses, i.e. 'FLOAT' 'DYNAMO', 'FRAILTY' 'DIVIDES' to name a few that deal with the crude realities of Life, Love and Death. It's real— a path, a diction, a lesson that readers may choose to follow in their lives.

I believe; this is the way the world can work: living with a focus, stumbling, yet! Still marching on the razor edge of life's journey to find and fix a nice goal, but this too can be a way of life as well and can lead to a life; that is full, rich, and fulfilling, despite the fact that, too often, we feel pressured by the voices, both external and internal on the way to accommodate all those, living and loving, till it tolls. I am sure, the readers will both enjoy the poems, and the collection will be popular and will get good critical acclaim too, which will encourage Mr. Samal to come up with more such volumes. I wish from the core of my heart, that success, be the hallmark of this volume.

Thanks

Dr. Sachidananda Panda
Asso. Prof. [English]
BBSR, Odisha, India

PREFACE

The Sermonic Verses: 100 Sonnets on Life, Living, Love and Death. The book has four Parts and carries 27, 32, 25 and 16 sonnets in a sequence from part one to part four. The sonnets have been modeled upon the Shakespearian form of 3 quatrains and a clinching, rhyming couplet. The sonnets are marked by deep introspection and absorbing reflection and cover a wide range of human experiences besides other elements of life, i.e. ethics, spirituality, philosophy and ratiocination. The use of 'Sermonic' in the title underscores moral overtones as well as the undercurrent of didacticism, skillfully embedded into the artistic frame of communication, leaving nothing explicit on the surface. The sonnets look into various aspects of contemporary life and the conflict of man today vis-a-vis his challenging circumstances. The reader can expect to find Shakespeare's range of experience and observation, Donne's unconventional metaphysical conceit, Browning's artistry, Wordsworth's natural flow of the verse with simplicity of diction, Frost's simplicity of expression, Auden's wit, and Coleridge's glorification of love.

The real appeal of the book lies in its unique description of life and death as a divine realism, and love and living as a spiritual journey toward humanism. Sometimes, the sonnets rise up to catch the reader in an unguarded moment and impinge on his conscience. Moral sermons that are critical of wrongful living and influential revolutionary content promoting true living constitute the two counterbalancing facets of many sonnets. An attempt has been made to present an authentic and dignified tone of the sonnets while depicting the complexities of contemporary life. In some sonnets, Volta is found after the 2nd quatrain or the 3rd quatrain in some other sonnets; and yet in some other sonnets, Volta does not appear but twists become palpable. With the three - the Theological, the Metaphysical and the Positive, the denouement of the 'couplet finish' is what enforces the specialty of the sonnets.

CONTENTS

Love

Death

LIFE

SONNET- 1
THE LIMIT

The growth of life buoyantly bears the womb

(And would bear ever), but can't hold the weight

When strikes the labor, then puts in the bosom

A cute offspring-- the Creation's wondrous guest.

The bosom laps the glory up with surge

Of love and keeps onto the breasts to suckle

The elixir, as the hands and hearts do nurse

The blest little thing with love and oracle.

But can a life which grows to stray be nestled?

And like the womb, the bosom too gives in

To toddler's forward impulse and does yield

It to the world to grow by its design.

Alas, none grows past the plan of the sphere,

And in its vagaries, each one does wither.

SONNET- 2
LIFE IS EDIBLE

See the ant-eater's body being eaten by ants!
If you can't mean, do look around and see
In platter of rebellions lie tyrants,
And Venus trap to eat the robber bee!
Yet see the falcon's vice to feed her chicks,
And more, the hungry hippo's brutal twist…!
Endo's or exo's, all are cannibal freaks--
Down the dinos and Neanderthals' list.
Life, mine or yours, is sweetly eatable--
Each being a consumer, 'so goods and wares;
Birds, animals, plants, humans-- all dependable
Do live on others and, too, die to others,
For, life means eating as well as being eaten--
Preys, predators, are all-- overt or hidden.

SONNET- 3
THE LAP

They came all with their lap, 'midst merriment,

To live and let all live by what's ordain'd,

And rush'd on, each subjected to own extent;

Some broke through, some in their limit remain'd.

The times of past did house them all,

But gone are they with times, one after one;

The past is dead in pyres and burial,

Each lap completed with end of the span--

The span that's transient on death expires,

As ends your lap if well-perform'd or ill;

But liberated you're from what transpires,

This is alone to God yours do reveal;

That, deeds of yours, if virtuous and austere,

Are placed on the lap of God forever.

SONNET- 4
THE FLOAT

I, fathomlessly, scan the bottom if
On prop of God does stand this universe,
Then, up into the heaven peer I if
It hangs by strings from His artistic fingers:
Depth in dark and height in glare do show
There's nothing yon the bottom and the top,
Like a balloon does float the Whole no tow,
As Nothingness has got it swallowed up--
The facts, the fictions, all inside the Unknown,
And wanders a tiny drop of human knowledge
In the ocean of bottomless and topless Creation
Attach'd no way to Acrobat's appendage;
And life grows, dies, in this undying gymnasium
Whose levitation-suspension's a conundrum.

SONNET- 5
FEAR

I bear in mind the moment I was tugg'd

Out of the fortress of my mother's womb,

When, by some trepidation, I was rock'd

If outside held me in the arms of doom--

The light, the sound, the touch, the whole unknown,

Uncanny open if, in a sinister siege,

Deprived me of my mum's impregnable haven,

Till she hid me in her skirt's comfort and ease.

Since then have I examined my inborn fear

And know it comes-- comes with ingress of each tik

Of time that our irrational mind's un'ware--

With surging threats yet more obscured, more bleak:

Unguarded moves our life, unsure and naive,

As fear overwhelms us from cradle to grave.

SONNET- 6
COLOURS OF LIFE

Doesn't life adorn itself with hues to show

As it does grow to an ego-vested soul?

And say if you do not know this self glow

Does belong to the spirit of the whole,

And paints of life by livers of the earth--

In myriad notes of visions and, too, vagueness--

Do carry facts real that pour down from birth,

With sketches vocal of Nature's genuineness?

Life is subjected to the Whole that owns,

Though lone all way through goes from fun to fear;

All portraying touches of emotional crayons

Deliver an image the life does bear.

And portraits of each distinct bloom and blot,

That, after death of beings, some fade, some fade not.

SONNET- 7
DYNAMO

The grave of past has held each corpse for yores

And swells as each one falls from living guild,

If universe sustains on lives of ours--

Grown and consumed for its superior build.

Emerge do lives from nowhere, beaver 'way

All through to self-aggrandize with their piles,

But sink into Nether and melt away

Fore'er, stripp'd of things earned by rights or guiles.

Life is, to guess, an action manifest--

By lot ordain'd by cosmic automation--

On move with each stage run that comes to rest,

Continually in some benign direction;

For, static's NOT the universe we live in--

Momentum gain'd with momentary propellin'.

SONNET- 8
THE SPOILER

If humans are what their mind makes them of
Or, like non-humans, form'd of earthy matters--
Too subtle a fact to find-- there's myth enough,
As we do rise and fall, so do all others.
Yet, lives of kinds we own do fairly tell
The human mind ain't engineer'd to change
The cogwheels of the life's cradle and hell,
Rather fill'd with a genocidal melange,
While plants and plumage, honeybees and herds,
All flourish side by side in peace and quietude--
Unterminated e'er their shared accords--
O'er the arty mind of human multitude.
And mind that constructs as well as destroys life
Is worse than theirs sans mind, malice and mischief.

SONNET- 9
HOMINIDS

Can things the mind aches for sustain the base
Of life all 'long the body does traverse?
How when the lustful mind devours the hapless
As live the elite on their blood, toil and tears?
You see your problem in comforts to own,
So, you can't see the problem of another
To get a loaf of bread thrown off your glutton,
So, block the recourse for food to starving hunger.
The sprouts of human wants desires do tend--
Synthetic all and weed through modern mind
Of block of vagaries, that floats to cursed end--
And grow them to models of a baleful kind.
Under the civilized cloak, all are aliens;
Possess'd with hominids are all homosapiens.

SONNET- 10
FRAILTY

Sometimes you look up to others, in esteem,
How heads of theirs are rising to the stars;
Sometimes 'so yet, you look down upon them
Those who've been flatten'd to the feet of yours.
But looking straight at your own life you see
Nor height nor depth, but on guardless flotation
That it is drifting toward death, precisely,
Enroute a devious course of fluctuation.
Life for you is what to you is visible--
Beyond the difference of a king or pauper--
That, within, it is purely frail and breakable
To plagues, pile-ups or swords of misadventure...
We see each other with whatever view,
But none is constant-- neither I nor you.

SONNET- 11
DIVIDES

I've grown among my bloods, neighbors, and mates,
And seen all-- same of body, bones and bearings,
Same humans of true virtues and same cognates
To one another, sharing same belongings.
But all this oneness, like a tattered necklace,
Has broken into fragments of odd mobs
By vices of trendy fads and meanness
Of modern day arena's cut-throat hubs.
Can journey of the living earth be boss'd
By humans rip'd apart with diverse dreams?
Aimless is life's progressive course, as toss'd
Up life's existence by our straying memes...
Men are men-- one class, women so equate:
God's two Divides; each else a fake syndicate.

SONNET- 12
IN THEIR LIMIT

Do you take note of humans rolling in filth,
Subsisting on means of their tireless labors--
Deprived of the elements of life, with kith--
And swarming in morass of urban gutters?
I do, and see their beaming smiles e'er ain't
Less glorious than light of the sun and faces,
Laced with impressions pastoral and quaint,
Less serene and genuine than heavenly graces;
So feel their soulful heart in love with things
They have as gifts of God, as they do sight
Modern desires as endless sufferings;
The day denying not food and peace the night,
In paradise of life, they stately inhabit
With limitless bliss, in fief of their limit.

SONNET- 13
THE FLOW

From height of mother's womb, comes out the flow
Silent and small, with a resolve to conquer
Life's insurmountable hurdles and to grow,
By right or might, to fame of no-feud victor.
Contain'd within its banks, it rushes on,
Passionate past rocks, over cliffs it falls,
Then wide it spreads out in a stately fashion
As banks recede and sink numberless thralls.
But, true, a river never rises up
And, though in aid to some lives and livings,
It only drowns the lows, earth masses and humps,
But flees mountains and hills in abject yielding
To finally flow to where it wished to be,
And, noiselessly, it merges in the sea.

SONNET- 14
LIFE IS GONE

I see all plants bemused, and e'er at peace,

With their genuine submission to the union,

And birds, in flocks and flights, e'er in bliss:

With foliage, with flaps, both live in true communion.

And I haven't seen when they slump, when they soar,

As all the past long they've been existing

By me since birth, but have not faded ever

Their youth and mirth, while I have reached my passing.

And ere my death, with tears do I repent:

Why I long'd for my me-alone-none-else self

And vices I grew in me that did dent

My life to death-- in isolation, no help!

Whence did I come and whither will I go?

But, chance of human life I spoilt, I know.

SONNET- 15
LIFE'S AN ABSTRACTION

Life, to know, does never end at grave,

Nor in the pyre is it consign'd forever--

Unlike body Nature does in it stave--

For, life isn't made of mortals which do molder.

Unbound of break-free cells and elements,

Life is not form'd, decomposed, or re-form'd;

Neither does it abide in carnal fitments,

Nor, like an object, is disown'd or own'd.

But, it's a stateless canvas of our mind

Which we do paint with colors of emotions--

Thick or runny or whatever kind,

But it has e'er remain'd yond definitions--

Beyond the touch of mundane existence,

Unhurt, unentertain'd, by our experience.

SONNET- 16
FOR THE NEW

Crawls the caterpillar for the case

To come out as a new born butterfly;

Or, for a noble pretence, does wriggle endless

The snake to shed its skin that's dead and dry.

The plant, so, lies whole year, in wait for Autumn,

To change its leaves and wear a shinier foliage,

As Nature's each elapsing momentum

Does life 'together cast off for a new lease.

That, putting on the present is like dying,

For, shifts the time e'er with the growing earth

And dry the wears away, in long waylaying,

Due for life to sustain with each new birth.

Rolls on the cycle of life with love for the new;

Though go the old, the new-- me after you...

SONNET- 17
RESILIENCE

Each time your leg is pull'd, you drag ahead,
But stop not, and each time your valued goal
Kicks you on the nose, you feel not dead,
But like the landed boxer, spring from fall
Back to the bout. Your love to lord the ring
Revives you fast, and thus you grow, re-grow,
Each time you drop; you never give up winning
However big is the loss and the blow.
Unstoppable is life, with fortitude
Pulling it on relentless 'long its track,
By resilience, as human aptitude
Delivers when our foes do pull it back.
Thus, life goes on absorbing shocks and barriers,
And grows more tolerable, thanks to winners.

SONNET- 18
THE OLD ARE GOING

The old are going-- their life at finish line--
No musing if they made it to the Stand
Or lagg'd behind those others who did shine
In limelight of their unique feats and brand.
Their shriveled face, hollowed eyes, fallen teeth,
Let them not pull out their nerves either way;
No curse, no oath, no laughter underneath
Their tattered lips or grief on deaden'd eye.
With final ink of tawniness fast fleeing
Their hugely claim'd life of immortality,
They pray to get rid of dishonor of dying
And quietly flee the world of mortality...
They're going. Let them go, wreath on for their soul;
Let truth of life define us and our goal.

SONNET- 19
RING IN THE NEW

It's no nonsense, if you rang out THE OLD

With lots of feasting, funning and fanfaring,

In frenzy of mind if you screw'd stranglehold

Round the neck of fail'd year till its dying.

No joke, if now on carcass of the dead,

You swear the new will be famously yours,

For, in our will is our Lady Luck made,

As builds up firmly a vanquishing force.

Alas, die away all on this very day--

Our oath, our spright-- like surge of smoke after blast,

As daily fiends of own do squarely flay

Our life, and future, through the year does last…

Let our gifted life deliver its due;

With will to change us, do ring in THE NEW.

SONNET- 20
THE DESIGN

Birds are chirping gay in boughs of spring
And men are splitting waves in wild excitement,
Mindless of others in throes of fate, dying,
Or over patriarchs, death being fiercely bent.
Lost are all in worldly existence,
In self-indulgence for physical pleasure;
Listless are they of life's divine essence
And of the inevitable, they're unaware.
That, they'll soon be replaced by novel creatures;
The heady birds, the hysterical men--
All transitory as mundane residers,
But to know God's design, they're too inane.
That, we come and we go-- all on the trot--
With God's each breath in and His each breath out.

SONNET- 21
TIME'S CUTTING WHEEL

With light and life alongside comes the morning,

Then hurry past all solar spells in turn;

Goes light, goes life, as Time moves past the evening,

All back to darkness and same ne'er return.

In dread, I try to hold back fleeing Time,

But slips it from grips of my mortal hands

And cuts through each that blocks its way, by whim,

Giving none a chance as it runs errands:

It wounds, it heals, it makes a king of you,

And a pauper of a king, no care;

And as it gets the day change its last hue,

All at the fall of the night fall dead-- all bare…

Spinning with vanes is Time's galloping wheel;

It takes each gain, so takes each pain, with each kill.

SONNET- 22
LOVE FOR LIFE

Who knows not truths that one day we will die
And life is more brittle than the house of cards?
As bubbles grow and burst, who can defy
The quirks of life or can have deathproof guards?
Eternal, yet, to live does throb each heart
While death does prey on others, on all sides,
Or when its troops ambush to drown each yacht
With wrecking blows, no look whoe'er that rides…
Lucky, the undying will of life does wonder
As it does rumble roughshod over death
And many legendary relics weather
Through time's interminable deadly path.
For love to live despite mortal vagaries,
Humans do make myriad immortal histories.

SONNET- 23
FEAR OF LIFE

The past alarms me in each lonesome moment,
Recounting horrors of human-made acts--
From my friend's death in a freak accident
To my teacher's, in slumber, by his son's bat:
Fear from within, fear from outer side,
Does stalk our life no relent, no relief;
To nowhere life does usher us to hide,
And bared to looming death is life's each leaf.
From shelter of chanced ease, watch I in dismay,
As draconian life makes each morrow harsher;
With death betiding us by sudden foray,
Why save, why boast of and why compete for?
Subjected are we all to our own bane,
As holiness of human birth goes in vain.

28

SONNET- 25
THE STREAM

Life is flowing with time ceaseless ahead,
As its each flow encounters the strangely new;
Adopt, adapt or confront them hard-headed,
It, in your fancied form, will never pass through.
No fact if you're a pro or playing about,
You are floating in the ebb and flow,
And suffer rugged pain when dry in drought,
When rain casts you out to racking alien powe(r).
Down the mainstream or staling in backwater--
By banks of sand, crag, mound or muddy mass--
Is caught your life, since you were sourced out ever,
Sea bound, and may, en route, away will pass…
Flowing is time. Do flee or fall or flow on;
All's momentary-- from and back to the Creation.

SONNET- 26
THE MORTAL LINKS

Whoever knows not that they all came

And, with passing of time, they all went--

With their acts, with their disrepute or fame--

Leaving all things they by their names meant?

Mahatma came with torch of peace and freedom

And pass'd away with the egress of time;

Had come Genghis with dreadful deaths and mayhem

And perish'd into grave with cruel regime...

Come the good and come the bad, in turn,

In Time's conveyer course that carries all

And throws them off when out they run

Of their breath, their body, their relay and role.

Goes on life on earth with ours living and dying--

Each being a mortal link of curse or blessing.

SONNET- 27
LAUGHING AT LIFE

I do laugh at my life some time or other
And 'so see on your face the kind of grin,
Of waves of scorn, or laughter I do hear,
If life as a joke you take on your chin.
Smirks up the pauper's wryness on his dry lips
As he drags back to hovel with empty bowl,
Or grimace when the erstwhile model peeps
Onto her crumpled face once all did drool'.
More, can your life be grave while Saviors fall
To shots of sinners or their sabotage?
Or, can there be a better satire at all
Than when your child disowns your parentage?
The whole of life echoes with sounds of laughs,
And clear when quiet are parties, pains, their flaps.

LIVING

SONNET- 28
PAINS

Pain of bones, of muscles, of organs,

And pain of mind from losses, woes, or wants--

We bear some, from some we get no riddance;

Some heal, yet some bring back more malignants.

Pain of penance still on ourselves inflict

We, and pain wreak'd on by the force of foes…

All pains do cleave to the life from birth to crypt,

Their roars being heard from human cries and lows:

The life that's pleasure-bent suffers from pain,

For, pleasure is fatal that has mortal pact,

And pains do ever spare no one insane

With body's lasting as an absolute fact;

And they inflict on us more suffering,

More we depart from Laws of simple living.

SONNET- 29
WHERE'S THE END ?

Where is the end of humanity's race

Our parents have made us run for, and what

Will we depict the future for the chase

That our children will take up for their lot?

Look down and see: D'you find a base beneath

Your feet-- the base legendary strides of greats

Had aim'd? Ain't their footmarks entomb'd in filth

Of beastly vices and inhuman traits?

All hopes the past nurtured are gone in perils

Of present-- be it bombs, bugs, crimes or climates.

Whither the present life? is what it grills

While caught are we by modern syndicates.

Ahead we see there's many a puzzling bend,

How can we promise us a heaven at the end?

SONNET- 30
DESIRE

The mind, in cell of self, feels not the bliss

Of freedom, its delights, in dark confinement;

But the enlighten'd, free from avarice,

Do get all zest of life from little, being content.

Insatiable hunger of mind is desire

Which leashes you to utter subjection--

Your craving suctioning you tighter ever

To resistless enslavement and abjection.

The human bent acquisitive that runs,

Feels not its friction 'gainst inherent objects

Of truth before it into ashes burns,

Yet, it ne'er its own fatal path rejects.

The more illusive charm inflicts more pain,

While a small glebe's all stars, moon, sun and rain.

SONNET- 31
CONQUEST

The yawning cracks of ice threatens to swallow,

As leaning crags will any moment crash;

But faith is climbing up with each axe blow,

Dauntless, and evils tamely allow the pass.

The victory point bobs up on mountain top

With Climber's courage bloating further yet,

Soon there will fly the winner's flag and flap

The glorious exploit deep down the State.

A snowy storm, all of a sudden, down does bear

And hits the mounter with its rocky squalls,

But tight his faith and grit holding together,

Sneaks 'way the storm 'neath his victorious smiles:

Courage that carries faith does glorify life,

Whereas fear does effect a fatal trip.

SONNET- 32
ENVY

I am what I am, till not you inflict
On me a shock with your feat of distinction;
'Worthless!', till someone in me does indict
Me, when I disdain my own recognition.
An overwhelming envy shatters my shape
Into a shapeless ghost-- 'lone in the planet
Of facts, desire, fulfillment, love and kinship--
More I look at your feat, more wither'd I get.
But envy has its magic of advantage
Which soon tricks me to dust the instant of shock;
My bouncy ego breaks through heaps of wreckage
And head in heaven, I stand as strong as oak.
I look down on your feat with mine a lot;
I am what I am, envy me or not.

SONNET- 33
BLOOD

Can't you e'er go beyond the hold of blood?
I wonder if your blood does thickly bear
A tincture of a 'chauvinistic code',
That is, the original ovule of Nature!
So, with the Nazi-mad fanaticism,
You spill blood of the non-blood with élan--
A bid, by your campaign of hateful schism,
To rid 'your earth' of the contagious clan...
How can you hold the absolute hierarchy
'Gainst streaming of the Eve-and-Adam myth,
Or spreading of the Darwinian reality,
While blood itself perceives not fair or filth?
Humans are we all– with blood of the eons--
The hybrid of the conjugated clones.

SONNET- 34
GREAT SOULS

I've question'd myself many times if soul

Is looking to me with any desire

And tried to understand its veil'd hyperbole,

Which stirs me up against my being off-flair.

It's so complaining of being sedentary

If to the nothingness of wilds withdrawn,

But rides composed so long as wings of glory

Are soaring high unpaused, untired, ungiven.

Rapt if they all listen'd to the cry

The ambitious soul of theirs would tensely make;

So voyaged victorious to limitless sky,

Their passion-laden will did stars in rake:

The insurgent soul does fire instincts for fame;

A great soul always goes with great name.

SONNET- 35
IN TRUE SHADE

The leaning boughs of great souls spread the shade

Of kindness, love, truth and non-violence,

That, under canopy of holy crusade,

Sustains the planet's human existence;

While rocketing of selfish growth does rise

In one-upmanly, defiant course to heaven,

But hell to which decompose all vain-glories,

Pull'd down by forces of the Leveling Bane.

The loftiness of virtuoso, stranger

To common good, bears not humanity

That seeks the civilizing shelter under

The true soul's lush foliage of charity.

There's hardly any that bows not to one

Who tends in him the soul of a true human.

SONNET- 36
AFTER THE BEAUTIFUL

The cosmic incidents 'cross the endless skies

Do catch our fancy and soak'd-in attention;

With earthy blooms, berries, and butterflies,

Make us fall for this beautiful Creation.

Billows and snowy brows of heavens height

Or woods, waterfalls, and oceanic whirlwind--

The livings and non-livings-- all that bright

And bucolic are drags for our opress'd mind.

The more we notice the Nature's allure,

The more devotional become do we

And more, like current of retreating river,

Do flow to beauties from daily ennui.

And more our livings get obscure and dirty,

The stronger gets our quest for each beauty.

SONNET- 37
BEING TOGETHER

Like clouds in windy sky together we get,

Then drift away from one another own ways--

In search of life the clique could not beget,

Or driven by winds as they change their passage.

By will or 'gainst, ripped our togetherness,

That, one's survival, being subsumed in self,

Fits, like free radical, in anywhere else

To fulfill one's desire or get, at risk, help.

Yet, strength of union that each of us bestows,

Like beauty of each bloom makes up the garden,

And like blooms we must in submission muse

The wellbeing of all. But, alas, a bane,

It's always been own interest or fear,

It's always been a business or a barter.

SONNET- 38
BEING CREATIVE

Birds go for foods and mates, so do animals,

And they have gone for everlasted years,

But all remain the same through springs and falls,

Though guts all fill'd and body in full cheers.

But the entire trail of their routine outings

Is soil'd with carcasses that don't evolve--

Through changes; ages gone but same in nestings,

Same life, same skin, same wing, same dog, same dove.

And succumb they to chances or survive,

Or live to end no cares, no thoughts, no plans--

Unlike we the growing humans who do live

With wish to colonize Cosmos with our clans:

Desire do we to transform life and death,

So we do create-- cross the heaven, cross the earth.

SONNET- 39
TEARS

Who dreads not fire the most when it is swallowing
Woods after woods? And who revels not the most
When down the floating reserves begin pouring
Water that saves the lives, their woody host?
Burn does human anger, like wildfire,
And in that fire are ashed both burnt and burner,
While tears like flooding torrents douse the pyre
Before the both men that its flames do smother:
Anger devours its prey, or stumbles on
Its tough begetter, conceding defeat,
When breaks the bank of sorrow and affliction,
Releasing tears to cool the mortal heat;
The bigger's wound, the stronger tears do flow
And stop not till they float you 'way from woe.

SONNET- 40
SONGS OF LIFE

Laments of loss in poignant elegies
Or hymns of thanks in prayerful submission,
The soothing charms of mother's lullabies
Or anthem of nation in pure oblation:
Songs are sung in many a mood of mind,
In many a rendering of streams and flows,
Life does utter where soul it does find--
Freely through croons or hums and highs or lows.
And notes of songs with tears or joyous refrain
That's solemnized with the spirit of oneness
Can sink a desert with deluge of rain,
Can melt mountains, can resurrect the lifeless.
And songs that sing the paeans of humanity
Are waved through vibes of earth to eternity.

SONNET- 41
MY WISHES

Up heavenward held have I my sight, and ponder:
'Can't I rise to the stars and pluck a lot?'
That, wretched earthlings in return for honor
Of me, will cuddle home, one each, of my unique stunt.
But fear soon shrouds my stuck-out visage of
The fantasy of Quixote, dwarfing me
To humble limit of this mortal stuff,
That, God of a human, I can't e'er be.
In falls and bruises is written my past,
For, often have I jump'd for the impossible;
And as I wake up ere few years to last,
I know I've lost the value of the possible.
Yet, with each passing day, more I become lame,
The height of wishful hope goes higher for fame.

SONNET- 42
BODY AND MIND

In tranquil moments of the Yogic silence,

I find the breath and mind of universe;

And with beats of gymnastic resonance,

My organs form all-powerful Godly force.

That, I spread through like water, air and light,

Through the inanimate and the animate;

With muscles of angelic wings and spirit,

I visit whole cosmos with speed and spate.

When sojourn ends, out flow of me in great hunt,

Hatred, lust, anger, greed, all Yamic sins,

As I step out into my daily stunt--

For conceit, mastery, possessions and wins;

The fate of never-dying body and mind

Is ground by fiendish teeth of mundane grind.

SONNET- 43
UNCLE MOON

My mother didn't, nor any other's did,
Who promised to pluck me that welkin lily,
But later I forwent my mother's bid,
For it was not a bloom, but my uncle only,
Called Moon, in beaming color of cream white,
Who lived in cheery sky with many toys,
And would alight, with wings of wind, some night
To take me thither for avuncular joys...
Though now false is each folksy lore or lyre,
We idolize our mothers, for the wisdom,
Who show'd us dream and farm'd in us desire
To scale the humanity's second home;
That, ere we lose love, lilies, life on here,
Depart will we for 'Chandmama' forever...

SONNET- 44
IN JAWS OF DEATH

Death is employed-- against killing, for killing--
From one to twenty, twenty to two hundred ;
Goes on deployment, goes on slaughtering,
Unresisted, undeterred, unabated.
All with attacks, defenses, counter wraths,
Has world now turn'd an ultimate war zone;
Pile up slain bodies, flow the floods of bloodbaths
In 'butchers-all-butcher'd-all' competition.
Humans are all-- who kill and who are kill'd--
In different designs, for different aims,
With horrors of homicides thickly fill'd
In combats, crusades, war fares, terror flames.
Bullets do spray above, beneath bombs and mines,
And caught are we securely, all, in between.

SONNET- 45
NAKEDNESS

The drag of modern-maniac artifice

Is so enamoring to sense appeal--

So urging a pleasure of self-sacrifice

Is the spell of its torrid touch and feel,

That, in the limelight bask the frames no robes,

As all do worship, love and laud the sight,

While, at times, drops dead my heart, mind probes:

How savage passion gets well-bred ignite?

The wisdom lacks its voice to exude

Against regime of money syndicates;

With, by the day, the culture going more nude,

The humans grow all lustful like the primates.

The Neoliths, gone age ago, now return;

In nakedness makes wild love a rerun.

SONNET- 46
THE NUDE PARADE

From walls of Khajurahos and Konarks--
Paraded are the ancient vagaries--
To fads of modern humans and monarchs;
Renown'd as get nudists, their votaries.
From beaches to hot springs to spas to clubs,
Adams and Eves do proclaim sexuality
And voyeurs throng the teeming pleasure hubs
On rise with trendy bare-all vulgarity.
The conmen mint money through creative campaign
As screens and boards and bills sport nakedness;
And blind are we, 'so dumb, with none to complain,
While vanish cloths like clouds from sunniness,
While pornographs do hug each dame and dude
Crazy to see us nude, to show us nude.

THE ESOTERIC

Losses abound, sorrows abound, but success
Has e'er remain'd, for multitude, too dear,
Which rich do amass by hook or by duress
Or buy it cheap at loots robb'd of the poor.
Revolutions have risen, and buried then
In the treasonous graves of the crusaders;
The Flag does fly gloriously in each lane
In veneration of victorious looters.
Saboteurs plough through plural dupes and dummies
Too naive to know the play of mobocracy,
That, with the broken tissues of their own mummies
Does build up the plutocrats' democracy.
Free does run the Cog of the Esoteric,
With impunity crushes poor and public.

SONNET- 48
FRIENDS DO NOT AGE

My friends have aged, so have I with them,
But nor have they, nor I, why says my eye
If blind to read distorted form and frame,
Stubble grey and face shriveled, shrunk and dry.
We've stood like ageless trees, from depth of past,
With branches, boughs, foliage-- all evergreen;
In mischiefs, jokes, chit-chats is braced each part--
Years gone, same comeliness, same childhood grin.
And dread the 'age-eaters' in stress, fatigue, so on,
To invade our company of 'elderly boys'
If in the Paradise we've fallen and feed on
Ambrosia of juvenile jestings and joys.
Bless'd are we to be, each day, together;
Together young will we endure forever.

SONNET- 49
SO WHAT IF I DIED?

I panic when droop my eyes to sleep each night

If I should ne'er wake up to see next morning;

Yet desperate to escape from shaming light,

I do fight back to sleep no fear of dying.

So what if I did die, my being asleep,

Ere I return to deathly wakefulness?

Why live in glares with painful lasting grief?

Better is to lie in comforting darkness--

Forever like the numberless who've died,

Or die each day without being glorified souls;

What if some live love, care, riches endowed?

All shall be laid deep in darken'd grave holes.

Yet, hands of hope wake me up ere the dawn

To win through frustrating light of the sun!

SONNET- 50
REPUBLIC

Supremacy of people, whoe'er can alter?
Whoe'er can carry the load of the masses
If not Republic's mighty transporter
That never stops, never runs into crashes?
Goes on the journey of the Juggernaut--
Thousands of years is its progressive course--
And has destroy'd many a tyrant and despot,
With their empires, by public's ultimate force.
Born were apostles to e'er growing axis
To add to might of humanity's van
Of liberty, equality and justice,
That, from Athens, Socrates had begun.
And now, we all will lead the great Republic
To model each of our children angelic.

SONNET- 51
THE ELDERS' AWE

Loaded with a sense of separation,

Their face gets droplets of awe palpable;

And when resides a thought of union,

They dread denials of being responsible.

They can't pace them with youths running blind,

For fads of fancy in the luring Broadway,

With tools and tenets left far 'way behind,

Who fade into the race with frantic headway.

Impulses do explode the youngs in torrent--

The winning force's a deviating onrush;

Have fledglings of freedom, independent

Of feathers of wisdom, flown ever glorious?

The gap does go yet wider as to snap,

As youths are fear'd back into savage trap!

SONNET- 52
ONENESS

Behold I beauty of the chromatic bow--
The treaty of contrasts 'neath the blue azure,
What can equate this rare majestic show
Of various colors that designs this Nature?
Diversity defines the bond of Creation,
In odds are form'd the Supreme amalgam;
In differences lies dynamics of Union,
Each one is part of the Eternal Spectrum:
The home is home we lovingly belong
To differences for whole of us to survive,
Sorrows we share-- gains, jobs, and joys among--
With love for the ordain'd fragments we do live.
Religions, castes, classes-- all differences,
Like heavenly colors, are links of oneness.

SONNET- 53
INDIVISIBLE

I find my existence in my own labor;
None but me to my earning, to my yearning,
To my love for enjoyment of own pleasure
That I am bound-- unbroken from my being.
And happy me is at peace with all around--
In hustle-bustle of day, in dreams of night;
In fulfillment of me, the whole is found
Blooming, becoming, bounteous and bright.
Yet, when my form by any bit is shaken,
By kind of damage or deprivation,
The human being in me decamps and bane
I jump on with a violent rebellion--
Till I secure my form, flesh, blood and bones,
Or I consign my being to sins of demons.

SONNET- 54
FEEL NOT FOR ME

I'm worst a bloke-- to feel, to look, to hear;

In descent, color, caste, and in each kind;

A human being of me I do abhor

In all my eyes, my ears, my heart and mind.

Yet, I can't live if not on garbage stacks--

The civic wastes, for me, big assets' worth;

And with all verve, I carry in jumbo sacks,

The everyday source of my life and growth.

Feel not for me if you can't make me like you,

Let me be with my nasty companions--

Midst putrid dumps, from winter to the dew,

And die with my unheard unhappy moans;

Lest, like your scraps changing form, I should be

Recycled by God to be a human of me!

SONNET- 55
THE NOISE OF SILENCE

The upsara couldn't break the sage's prayer
With raunchy roars of her seductive anklets,
And thunders of a thousand drums did founder
To breach the soundproof ears of the demon's silence.
But the drop of a pin blows me into dust
Once gets sunk into quietude mind and body;
Sundry cants, quarrels, curses hard do burst
My head with Netherly cacophony.
And guilts and failures of my own combined
With shouts of greed from morning sun to streetlight
Do batter me, as eerie moans of wind
And canines chill the spine at dead of night.
Grows the noise of silence by the moment,
Through my desperate search for a restful quiet.

SONNET- 56
DEMONIC BLISS

I see a tiger tearing at the hind

Of an antelope young, with his cruel jaws,

As wretched prey looks here and there, resign'd

To its fate, under the man-eater's paws...

Like Taimur's bone-chilling savage parade

Or Hitler's exterminating of humans,

The bestial violence is thickly loaded

In our civilized brain and brilliance.

Can civic morals be a celebration

Of demons like Aghoris over corpses?

But blood-bent mouth knows not what to relish on,

For self pride, other than the weakling's flesh.

Go on the flesh-eaters' carnal festivals;

Go on the Quran-Bible-Gita's gospels.

SONNET- 57
I HAVE A HEART

I have a heart no different from yours--
In size, in make, in its perpetual toil
And rhythms of your life when you have nerves
And when in pride you swell, in pain you boil.
It, like yours, is so soft to touch and feel--
A charming crimson with sprays of scented zephyr--
When I behold you, your sweet eyes and smile,
That, it does smile in warming beats and measure.
Yet, sometimes, hard becomes the heart of mine--
A stone that has no ears, no eyes, no senses--
When it can't hear the cries of others' pain,
Can't see their woes, and when fall they, does rejoice.
I know not if your heart is so obstinate,
But, honestly, this heart of mine I do hate.

SONNET- 58
BEYOND THE SKIN

When heart is rapturous, when mind is blameless,
When thoughts that sacred go with dauntless faith,
When work is watery with sunshine wishes
And pollens of oneness, when flies my breath,
When words of virtues blow in lights of truth
And waves of strength, does flow my ardent will,
When hymns of humanity, sings my mouth
In rhythmic voice and with momentous zeal;
That, I do dwell in paradise of peace
Where I intuit, dream up, derive and create;
That, I do love, do serve for common bliss,
All I locate with, to all I relate,
When lifts me up the hands of Supreme being,
From worldly sorrows, pains and suffering.

SONNET- 59
IN MANY FORMS

To boundless sea with rivers do I flow,

Do glow with sun in spread of happy light--

Across the girth of whole surface-- and blow

With balmy wind on endless elegant flight.

I get the planet curl'd up into me--

Beneath my embracing nocturnal wings,

With starry eyes of the heaven I do see

If life is sleeping serene in Nature's nestings...

Thus I reside, thus I abide, and wander

In many forms-- formless of my own form--

My soul breaking free from the mortal cover,

As I'm absorb'd in Creator's Macrocosm.

And I feel not if I have got a birth,

If, some day, I will leave this mortal earth.

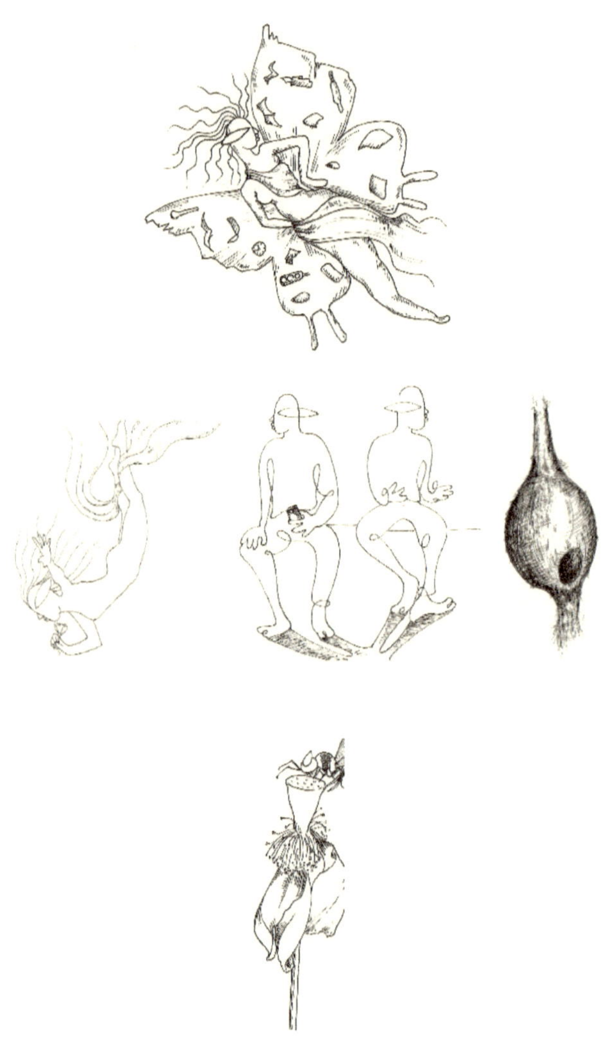

LOVE

SONNET- 60
THE BLOOMS

There grows a garden on the bed of peace,
Where frolic merrily the blooms of love;
In hearty communion, they effloresce--
Truth and piety within and smiles above.
With hums of humanity on all lips,
The whole gets radiant with floral delights;
In service of others where pledged are lives
Stack'd up with virtues, glow'd up in Godly lights.
And stand the blooms together proudly ever
Through ruthlessness of many falls and summers;
Unhurt, unbroken they play about in cheer
Through buffetings of many storms and raiders.
Invincible they grow in amity,
Will bloom forever they in gaiety.

SONNET- 61
LOVE FOR LIFE

Life is not just what you are made to deal--
By culture, conventions and rights and duties,
Or reading how pleasures and pains we feel--
But love in you for humans, birds and bees.
And love at peace with you is life attained,
But life is unattainable like the height
The sky presents, howe'er you trek and tend;
Enroute, love fades for some; for some, grows bright:
Inevitable are shifts in love, through stages,
As you ascend, when darlings upon you chance;
That, love you lose or love you gain on changes
Or love till death ferry you in a trance.
Whatever, life with love is e'er a fun,
While life sans love is blindness in the sun.

SONNET- 62
MADE OF LOVE

Life is design'd to live in anything,

Or all things at a time-- with love, of course--

In lives, non-lives, things we feel or feel nothing,

If there is Soul of God in universe.

There is no life where in love not resides--

Be it love for what transcends the mortal limit

Or like blossoms on a love-knot, briefly abides--

There's love always as natural legit.

But life possess'd with love for one and th' same

Is prisoning the self in a far-off isle

That nourishes the life till fall of the frame

Or proves too strange for self to stand the exile.

Yet, love is love as sacredness of soul;

Lovable are all-- from a grain to the Whole.

SONNET- 63
LOVE'S SUPREME

Now, on your head does fall the rain of boulders--
In tolls, denials or pitiless tirade;
Then in beatifying love, do breathe the showers
Of petals singing balmy serenade.
In pleasure you rejoice and buckle in pain
As through the chequer does your life go on--
Being held 'long crisscrossing of loss and gain--
By brace of love for something or for someone.
And love that holds your life may be as best,
Or odd and uncharacteristic, as you,
But love for life and life for love are blest
Together and, than God, more pure, more true.
There's a supreme soul in each one who loves
And each supreme soul is dearer than Heaven's troves.

SONNET- 64
LOVE AT 50

No strange when love captivates you at fifty,
Where the beloved is none else than a lass--
Her chanting voice, magical eyes, rare beauty
And body apsaras can't match en masse.
Some strange, the lass' latching onto you fast
And loving you if none else does exist
On earth. So is for you, your flying full mast,
Even death for her you find hard to resist.
But all strange when your love is never sexual,
Though your bodies and souls are bound together
Secure-- with her head on your pectorals,
Or your head at rest on the feet of her...
Thus sacred navigates the love strong blood
Between ageless goddess and ageing god.

SONNET- 65
STRIPPED OF LOVE

The lonesome soul does restless run in search

Of nest whose build incomplete yet, then, when

A stormy wind did blow it off its perch,

And since, has years gone by, it writhes in pain--

The wretched soul, in tears that run not dry;

Can crying over spilt milk be redeemed?

Yet, cries the soul, cries its abortive outcry.

It knows the ravaged nest can't be retrieved,

And knows, sans its nest never can it exist;

Yet, till death, it shan't cease the quest for love,

Though thrown down hard, wings broken; its tryst,

Though it knows, nowhere in the tree above--

Rich, luxuriant and beautiful yet more;

Its boughs with other nests and souls yet stronger.

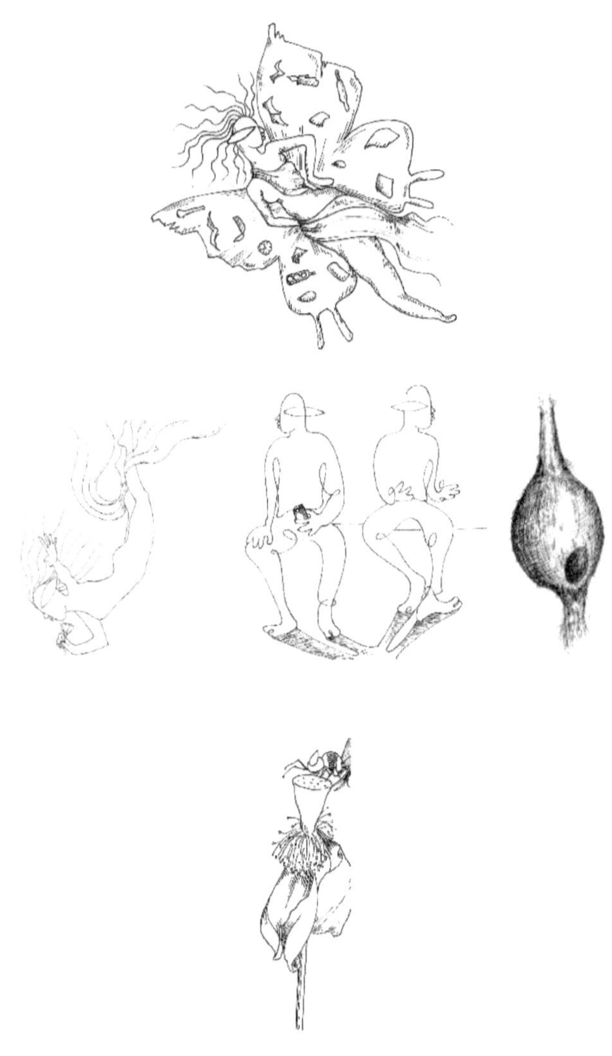

SONNET- 66
LOVE THAT ROARS

No doubt, the love that roars rebounds as hate

And plummets fast downward till it does smash;

The hell-bent maniacs spiral passionate

And roar in the air ere tragically crash.

The more the trekking goes up, more the love

Engenders hate, and summit of extremes,

Being uneven and steep, does disapprove

The lasting of the belligerent dreams.

Maniacal love, fatal no fail, does kill

The self, does fix the soul to an utter pain;

The table-top passion being blindly mobile,

Its over-shooting meets the fated bane...

Long lasts not love where vulgar show abides,

As each in the other's fate lethally resides.

SONNET- 67
THE DOLL WITH ME

Can e'er a doll abuse, dread, utter curses?
It can't to you till you have broken her dream,
Smother'd her freedom to express her sinless glees
And yourself posed as corrupted and mean.
Condemn me! Villain is none else than me--
For me, my Doll is sorely suffering,
And loss of grace and pain that's bearing she--
Condemn me! For my sin, my Doll is crying.
My Doll with me does hate me as the worst--
Doll of my daughter who will ne'er return
To this unfortunate, unfatherly ghost--
The loss I, till my death, will densely mourn,
With me at my Doll's feet till sinks the wreck'd yacht,
The causes of my sin buried in my heart.

SONNET- 68
RETURN OF THE DOLL

The heart-rending cry of a childless father,

From the deep of a solitary ocean--

Whoe'er can hear save the heart of his daughter,

And dare the seas to save the shipwreck'd human?

Alights the angel on godforsaken isle

(Not possible sans filial sacrament),

As rises up the moribund exile

Before he succumbs to self-banishment.

A father, when gets back his missing child,

Surprises God with his creative resurgence;

Yet, dazzled is his daughter of the yield

He's made for her even in her absence--

A wonder world of puppets, dolls, images,

Which mirthfully start talking with her touches.

SONNET- 69
LOVE AND TEARS

Are love and tears always compatible?
Unknown if each to the other well forbears;
But tested with a break-up in the middle,
There's no substantiation of love sans tears.
But tears do float you away from attachment,
Away to farthest brink of love's rejection,
Till you enter the ego of detachment
Which homes you safe in angst and indignation.
The more your ego rises, more your grief fades
And into sucking summery billows,
Entire pool of your tears evaporates.
Alas, when summer exits, autumn follows,
And soon return your tears in heavy torrent,
Each drop of it besprinkling your love's paint.

SONNET- 70
LOVE FOR A CAUSE

I wish'd love she requite-- in desperation,

But can a tree, which offers its shadow

To fagg'd pedestrians, need shade in return?

And so for love, I shouldn't sink to the low.

Up into me I look: Here lies the whole

Life for me, my foliage, my boughs and buds;

That, I exist not in my want, but in dole--

Light of the sun that he selflessly accords.

By grace of sun is molded life of mine;

So, by no virtue, I can be demanding,

For such niggardly handout for my Tzarine--

The shade which's sun's unselfish offering:

My love for her is what a shade just means,

This shade does go as evening intervenes!!

SONNET- 71
FORGIVE ME!

Death has sent me a missive of arrival

And I have drop'd whole stuff 'gainst sinking down,

But how to rise to heaven though robed off all?

My mind is heavy with your curses thrown.

I'm stewing, like fluid, on a burning stove,

Lest my ignorance has distress'd your being;

Forgiveness, lone recourse it does behove,

Will rid me of the burden of unwise sin.

That, on me, build up heaps of guilt and shame,

If I've wrong'd you with my misdeed and gaffe;

Even I consign me to immolative flame,

Or take penance, it won't absolve my self,

Won't rest in Heaven my soul if died tomorrow;

Forgive me now, lest, I mayn't see the morrow!!

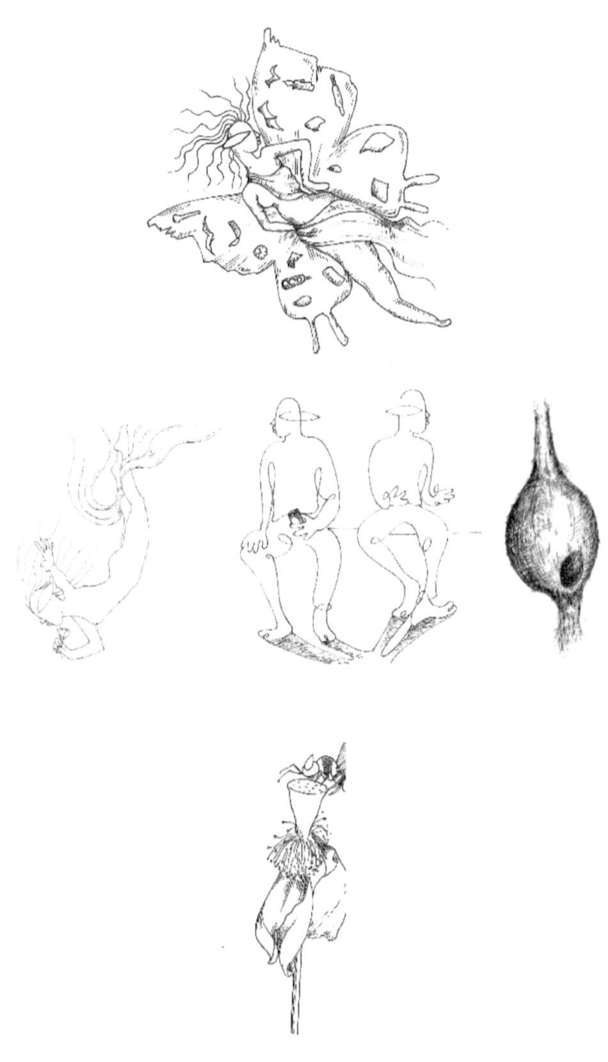

SONNET- 72
FEAR NOT TO LOVE!

Fear not if love of yours will one day be wreck'd
Off vessel and drown will you no help, forlorn;
Vessel may go, shan't you to die be left,
For, love is never friendless and alone.
E'er wakeful to save you are love's companions,
If ship did sink to navigational bane
Of maritime marauders, swirls or cyclones,
Or, like republics, cuddled a new captain.
Yet upon you, at first, rests on the fame
Of your love-sharing voyage that spoil you may;
But fret not, there are friends to take the blame
And lifeboat you across the troubled bay.
To name them are hope, hatred, tears and anger:
The four Samaritans of love-lost lover.

SONNET- 73
MY DOLL AND ME

What could well be more cheerful for a man

Condemn'd to die childless than the call of 'papa',

And more a grant, when voice is of a doll, than

The man's fathering woollen replica?

Revived and human'd I've been, by the doll,

With beatified parentage in a father,

If bred an angel, and down the unborn times all,

I will be farm'd up in my blood-- my daughter--

Whom with my pieteous grinds shall deify

Before my life's unalterable recourse.

A waning mortal I may some day die,

But shall not die my Doll and love of ours.

And with our father-daughter's holy image,

My Doll shall live on brighter by the age...

SONNET- 74
BETWEEN LOVE AND HATE

When struck with love for my unfaithful love mate,

Distress'd get I being dwarf'd, hers towering;

When I look down on her from height of hate,

My heart does lament, sympathy deep-stinging.

On one side, lies an agitated bay

And, on the other, limitless dark water,

And love can't take me ashore, or hate away

From death-and-life's unsparing rigid juncture.

At perils of to-be-or-not-to-be,

How long will I remain becalm'd more, if

I can't be a lover, nor can hater be,

Endless being afraid of death, afraid of life?

Thus I am: love revealing, hate beneath--

One threatening life, one ensuring death!!

SONNET- 75
LOVE THAT'S NOT

Has love of any two e'er been a success?

The question you can't answer sans a doubt,

For, human love is anybody's guess,

And none does know what love is all about.

Love, as a fad, has fallen badly flat--

The rich, the smart, all giving in to tripping

Of one-to-one romantic applecart,

For, runs not long the 'thrust-effected' outing.

(Can ever Siamese twins run long together?)

And spent is contact of two bodies fast--

Affection turning into sharp disfavor--

Each hungering the bonding off to cast.

Limiting can't be love to any two,

And boundless love comes not from bodies tied to.

SONNET- 76
HERS IN UNIVERSE

My eyes behold her 'cross the universe--
In forms and colors, in fiction and fact--
In her, do I discover its true source,
Resources-- things that lie and things that act:
Like stars she twinkles and like moon she blooms,
Like seasons she alights with fruit and flowers,
In streams she meanders, soars in flights of plumes,
Settles she deep in planet's blues and bowers.
But, wrath if now, then tears do grab my eyes
When her leaving of me does hunt me down,
As marvels of Nature with goods and glees
Do turn to ashes or in tears do drown.
Even so, eyes thrust out of each mortal burden,
For lifeful views of her in whole of Creation.

SONNET- 77
LOVE FOR HER

Ask me if my love will immortalize me,

I'll smile and quote a humor, 'Human's mortal.'

And ask me if timeless my love will be,

I'll mimic me, 'My love ain't monumental.'

Yet, if you ask me if I'll die for love,

'My love ain't selfless.', I'll no check admit;

To next-- if God of my love does approve,

'God and my love and soul always cohabit.'

If you still can't make out my love for her,

Time will show you a legend or a myth;

But, ask me not if she loves me as much, for,

I'll die from laughing and before my death,

You'll find tears in my eyes all visible

And hear my gasping voice: 'I'm not lovable.'

SONNET- 78
DEVIATION

Fast arousing physical impulses
Released the wild instinct of bestiality;
The holding sentinels of human senses
Defended the refuge of morality:
In between youth and aged ran my love--
Passion propelling, reason controlling;
In fuel of licit consciousness I drove
Along least trodden path, for balance, struggling...
On one side was the devil, God on the other--
One pulling me leftward, one pulling rightward--
I stood the tug ere I tumbled to former,
That ruin'd forever the love of this 'nomad'.
So tempting was the charm of the forbidden fruit
That I, no heed, did deviate from the route!!

THE TRANCE

A first, each time she comes and sits close by,

Her delicate hand on my thigh at rest;

A last, each time she says a piteous 'Bye',

Taking her nestled head off my upper chest.

Her sojourn blossoms with delights of smile--

The like of beauty and luster nowhere glitters;

Her charm-fill'd voice none else would so beguile,

That, her parting stirs up my woeful tears.

I kiss her hand with a drop or two

Before she sinks, into the unkind haze,

With all the splendors of the Himalayan blue,

And from my forlorn soul and flooding eyes.

Ensnared by the trance of infatuation,

I grope to mine the real from deep illusion.

SONNET- 80
LITTLE LOVE

I write an essay for one word she sends,
And a drop of her love does create an ocean
Of love in me, and my wait never ends
Hard though my prayer fetches her return.
Then jerks me up my phone with midnight call,
'What're you doing?' Before I make my babbles right,
She taunts and giggles, calling me 'a pagal',
And snaps the line with the parting shot, 'Good night!'
Her mischief tickles me, more than it does torment,
Though unrequited goes my love and care,
Though more to my woes, she n'er does relent
In teasing me on with her naughty affaire.
Yet, I do find my life in her each riddle--
The word, the moment, and her love albeit little.

SONNET- 81
LOVE AND KISS

The morning heaven, love-struck in solar dye,
Bends down fondly to kiss the innocent earth,
And she, proud of the fondness of the sky,
Does offer her coy cheeks in plenteous mirth.
Then, sun-and-earth's emotive parting kiss
O'er golden sparkles of oceanic splendor,
That spreads the true union's eternal bliss
Painted with natural love's twilight rapture.
But, sometimes, rapid come ravaging storms
And ruin the meetings of beauteous Creation;
More, our own sins, with many corrupt terms,
Do damage celestial love and affection.
Yet, meetings never end and end not kisses,
And true love ever blooms with holy incense.

SONNET- 82
THE VALENTINE PIG

Can ever a heifer take her pig home--
Her love-- though he, for hers, does wish to leave his?
Or, can the pig erase the creed and custom
And give in his, his love her high-born prestige?
Cries the pig as he intuits his failure,
Though he's forsaken poop and lives on milk;
He knows he's got the skin that'll alter never,
Nor for love's sake, must he defile her ilk.
Though wise he thinks, his heart pines for his cow,
For, he finds him in her soul, pleasure and pain;
Yet, for her pride, he mustn't go high nor fall low,
May he die lone to own grief and disdain.
Yet wonders he: Why God gave her, then split--
The loss more painful than his life's retreat!!

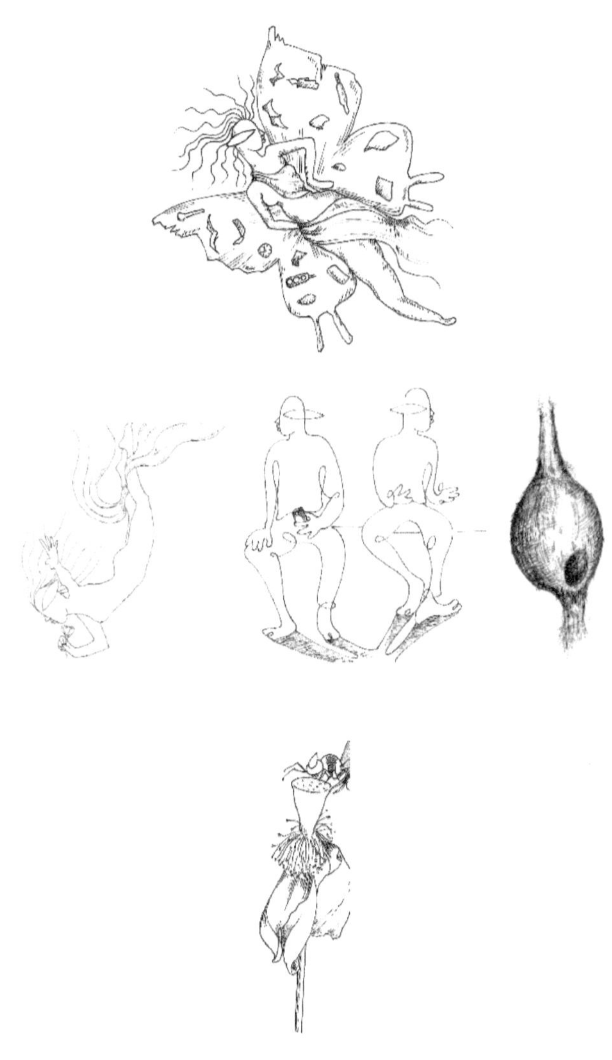

SONNET- 83
I DO CRY

I cry. I do cry breathless like a baby.

You notice me or not, but I do cry,

Whole drown'd in tears-- be it night or day it be--

No care if you find me absurd and wry.

But I can't be unfair to cry, or vague,

If crying can protect me from strokes of death,

Which nothing else on earth can, though I beg

Her comeback-- palms held heavenward, in good faith!

Yes, I do cry, (Whoe'er on earth will not

With the betrayer's dagger stabb'd in heart?)

But know my tears will flow all through the drought

And grow new plants of love ere life does part.

Haply, to get rid of fatal pain heart bears,

Come out generously life-giving tears.

SONNET- 84
THE CRYING DOVE

You came and left, if life you found in me
Too waste a place to host your saintly sojourn;
Howe'er long will this Jacobin's wait be
Ere you return, ere your showers return?
But I shall wait-- till my life does depart--
With sin of filicide of the mourning dove,
Like in her mourns as she tears her chest 'part,
Bangs her head for killing her own love,
That I do cry-- eyes dry, heart aching, hope wither'd,
As luck is lost with Cookie by an unfair take;
All nests are full of cheers, so is each bird,
But razed's my nest, unquench'd my thirsty beak
Held up open ever for your ingress,
Oh my daughter, my only blood and flesh!

DEATH

SONNET- 85
THE ULTIMATE

When death reminds me it will come-- a truth

Inevitable like setting of the sun--

I stare at life dumbly from North to South,

From East to West; a haze holds me forlorn!

Yet, desperately, I float through the girth--

Light years deep, but my travail hits no shore!

I look heavenward in awe, then down to earth--

Beneath my feet, but it's all death does roar!

What life could I measure if it's to set,

For good, opposed to sun that'll rise again?

Same sun fore'er-- same shape, glow, life and zest--

And I'm no more, neither my gain nor pain!

No count what I have got or will bequeath,

My life is short-lived in infinite death!!

SONNET- 86
NO DEATH

I dread when I behold the earth to come--

The earth o'er there, beyond you can imagine,

But I can see what the future does form--

A deathless, safe, sublime earth down the timeline.

And I dread I will die for good and all,

But all will exist with that earth forever--

The sun, the moon, the stars, the rain, the fall,

The blooms, the birds, the wild, the soil, the river--

All with benign earth of beauties and bliss

And, too, immortality, but I'm nowhere!

To death does each fall, no doubt I will perish

The soul of my body, self, pride-- all bare.

Mourn I born now to die before that earth

Where die will none once they've there taken birth!

SONNET- 87
DEATH THAT'S REAL

Death is not death that's brought on by the saber

Or when a virus causes life to fall,

Nor is it coax'd to venom of betrayer

Or press-gang'd into the abetter's cull.

Unearn'd, undone, is death that dies ere time--

The time ere fall, a fruit delivers seed,

As halt divine progression, chants of Hymn

And Holistic plans for which God does breed.

Each born does get a leg to complete it

And add to Creation for attaining death;

So, unattain'd as by the fallen spirit,

Befalls us God's fury, our fate underneath.

Death is death that crowns the Holy course;

Death is death that falls to Godly force.

SONNET- 88
THE VACUUM

Page after page, I turn back on my life

And see each day has past no words to show,

Robbed of are all of rivalries and strife

On every recto and on every verso.

No trace of tears, or bloodshed, or champagne

Of joy, as I pore over, does appear;

All feats and defeats of my selfish campaign

Are gone beneath the sheets' each rusty layer.

If, at all, from the depth, spurt out big ones,

Death in wait instantly sucks them down;

Superfluous life of gain and self-indulgence,

As into vacuum of the void, does drown.

I find in me no David or Goliath,

As slides the life into the abyss of death.

SONNET- 89
DOWN TO DEATH

You wish to run away from life, as gather

Its tests and trials with loads of frustration;

Then hits death head on your absconding humor,

And you bounce back with fright and trepidation--

Back into 'hell' where you can't live nor die;

For, there's no third home that exists beyond

The obvious-- in life, in death-- and lie

These heavens in living and in dying, no yond'.

Commandment bids: Live your life to the full,

Through built-in shares of shocks and sufferings,

And 'so accept death, it being the ordain'd rule--

Equally formulated for all earthlings.

And pains the more you get, the greater worth

Of Paradise death, for your soul, brings forth.

SONNET- 90
DEATH IS DIVINE

You hate to die as love for life builds up;
Your soul being serviced by the order'd Nature
And humankind singing your paeans atop,
On corpse of death, you wish to live forever.
How can, what God has order'd for Creation,
Creatures disown, denounce, de-canonise?
If life, as a fact, you licitly do own,
So death is no false either to despise:
Death is as sacrosanct as life reveals--
Irrelevant, ungot, is life without;
Salvation gets the soul in death when dwells,
For, the life that's for death remain'd devout...
Life for Experience, death for Resurgence;
Both life and death are parts of Providence.

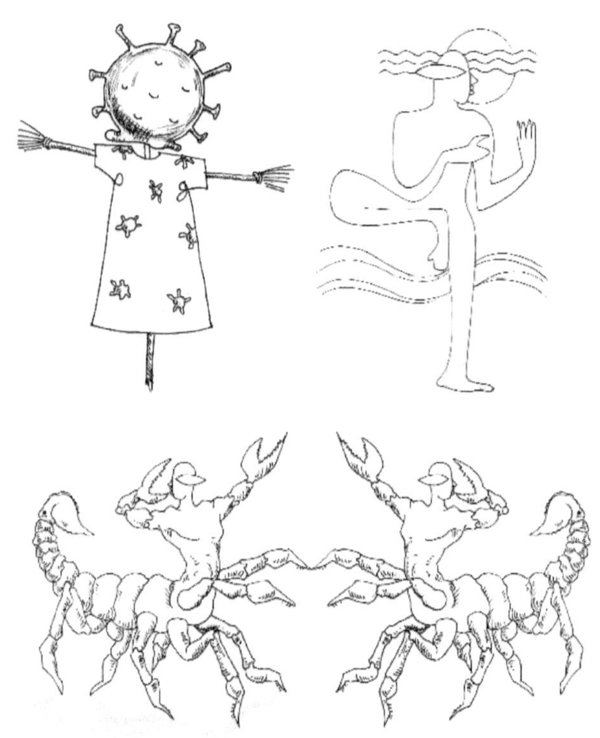

SONNET-91
DEATH DOES YIELD

The truth of death is never what you know,

That, it is one who forces you to perish

And robs you of all things you own and grow,

Your life, your honor, all you love and cherish.

But none of yours, in fact, is lost in transit,

As God redeems all things of yours on death,

That makes this 'delegated life' complete;

You rest in Heaven and lasts in God your breath.

Then, He does wake you up from your 'repose',

If He finds your work well redeemable,

And sends you back to earth and does impose

A new mission for The Incorruptible.

He gives us life for work and death for rest;

So life is, death is-- both at His behest.

SONNET- 92
DEEDS OF DEATH

Marauding march of death does trample all--
The plain, the high, the low, the dense, the open--
Unfailingly instant that it does fall,
As lightening strikes or trucks, or booms the gun...
Death spews fire, throws waves, or triggers quakes,
And die 'way kings, commons, foes, Samaritans,
And longer we grow, stronger havoc it rakes
If comeuppance get we the wretched humans;
So confused of ours being with truth or falsehood,
That we do act with co-destroying insolence,
As Nature takes its toll on ripe and crude--
Yet higher by the time, roused by our offence…
With us, evolves the incidence of Fatality
If we, for death, do compete with Almighty!!

SONNET- 93
DEATH DOES TRIUMPH

The 'self'-possess'd fanatics run the course
Of violence, vainglory, o'er the innocent
And wreck sore havoc on them, no remorse,
By force of money, muscle and armament.
Marauders do proclaim invincible
Are they. But, has it ever been proved so?
All powers of the mortal, formidable
However, crush'd are all by The Ultimate's Blow.
The might of death is mightiest of all mights;
From hell to heaven, dogs, devils and despots— all,
In graves, are buried whoe'er inflicted plights
And wish'd to hold the fortune of the whole...
Live as you may, but death does triumph always;
And a gospel forebodes this 'mortal presage'.

SONNET- 94
PEACE OF DEATH

Who thinks life is for pleasure knows not death,

That, one, obsess'd with comfort, wastes delight

Of death which life that's pledg'd to work does 'queath--

Like labor of the day makes up the night.

Life is the life of action sans ego

And dedicated in the name of God,

And with your lustfree spirit's workful brow,

You can imagine death's deathless abode,

That, death's the extended sleep you sleep each day--

The state of rest in perpetuity,

Your body lying all 'cross the earth and sky

And head in Heavenly lap of Almighty.

For each exhausted life, there lies ahead

Infinite peace in the Creator's Bed.

SONNET- 95
DEATH DOES TEND

I've fallen many times, but each time I've fallen,

Death has raised me with his immortal hand

And life's numberless deadly blows have spun

To fun by the touch of his magic wand.

The thought of death does resurrect my corpse,

Inspirit my soul and inspire me to rise

And brave the life's relentless jagged course,

And I walk 'gain no pain, no tear, no bruise.

With death holding a beacon up o'er yonder,

I notice, in that lighting, all do perish

Under his feet-- the evil, the good– forever,

My being left with no bias or grudge to nourish...

So, endure can I my plights, thus, submitting

To death's absolute bearing on my whole being.

SONNET- 96
RENUNCIATION

The raze of swollen sea to thunderings
Of monstrous clouds to quakes of withdrawing earth,
And pandemics to fatal human failings…
Whose life is it that dreads not face of death?
But death 'lone shocks the one who celebrates
The gains of body in absolute fashion,
For, life to death in matters sole relates—
The more possess'd one is, more trepidation.
And who renounces life of joy, collects
Pearls from oceans, stars from heavens and ever
Remains in transcendence-- beyond connects
Of fatal forces death does swiftly fire:
Renunciation is the embodiment
Of life-- unbeatable, undying, unrent.

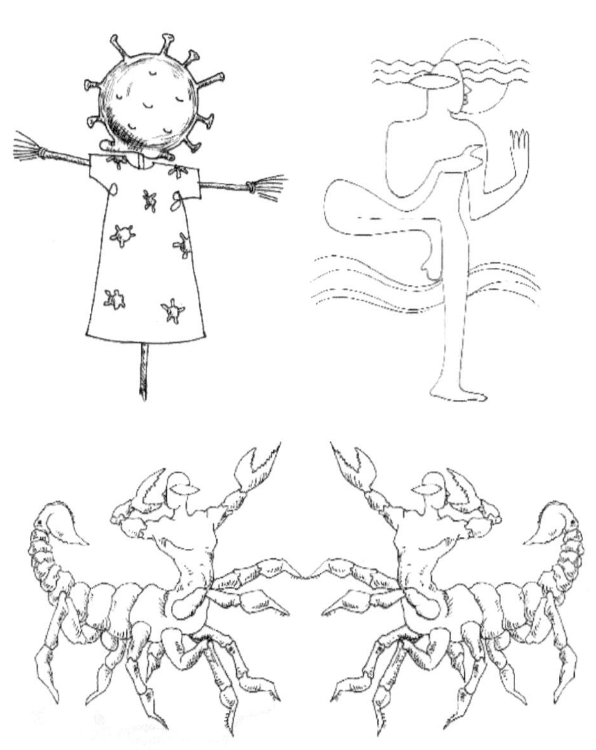

SONNET- 97
ON STEPS OF DEATH

Strange that death does rescue you from death,

But it does-- many times when life does wane;

Its helping hands pull you out of the depth

Of gloom, ferry you ashore the mortal main.

On steps of death does rise the life that's fallen,

Being vital 'gain by your eternal being,

The seer, immune to malign'd affliction

Of deprivation, sickness, disgrace and failing.

That, the death of the others who did rule

The life and consumed fortune by their sheer skill,

And that, the death they died ain't minuscule

Of wretchedness your life does deathly feel.

On each famed death, your death to life upends;

The mighty die; to the humble, death bends.

SONNET- 98
COMES LIFE, COMES DEATH

Comes the sun from night, to night returns,

Yet, darkness as abortive thrust of Nature,

Does, sometimes, terminate its diurnal course--

Light and energy breathes out sunset ere.

However, sun denies not its essence

To come and live the full day no alarm;

Thus comes each life with lease of permanence,

Though full or little, it forfeits its charm:

Life-- all an ardent glow, like firefly's moment,

In dark infinity's star-studded girth--

Does visit as insatiable mortal bent

And dies un'ware to vagaries of death.

Yet, death as life's inevitable companion,

No human should blaspheme or fear The Clarion.

THE DEAD DO NOT DIE

The extent of mortality's endless trail
Of humans that are dead ne'er lifeless lies;
Never are dead their values, valiant tales
Of success, their service and sacrifice.
Neither are they whose mortals fall behind
The walls of fame, for, life does climb each ascent;
For ever-growing lineage of the humankind,
The souls of all who die are ever present--
Some are embalm'd, some etch'd deep in our heart
And some, with beacons in cockpit of brain,
Do show us path of wisdom of the past
And, with the immemorial others, do flow in
Our life as blood and breath; in gleam and gloss,
The dead are never dead, but live in us.

SONNET- 100
DEATH UNDER NOSE

With awestruck eyes does stare about the scapegoat--
Once at the butcher and his busy chopper,
Then at its fellow beings who, on the trot,
Do perish on the block, but come back never.
Then looks around and sees the grins of humans,
Their caressing eyes, and, rid of fear, it smiles back--
The brainless animal-- failing to mean the nuance
Of human guile of mutton-for-green-stack.
It's grown in their care and protection from wild,
'Been fed on nutrition from fodder to farm,
That, they have raised it healthy and nourished--
Can it suspect amidst them any harm?
Lone cynosure of greed now revels in its life,
Though, on it, turns the butcher with his knife.

N. P. Samal, who teaches English in a professional college, is a versatile man. He juggles language, literature, law, social psychology, theosophy as well as administration with equal ease. Ever since he took to writing at the onset of COVID-19 in India, he has published three books in Kindle Amazon and three other books are going to be published in a while. His writings range from poems to school rhymes to essays to memoirs and moral stories for school children, etc.

THE SERMONIC VERSES

The Sermonic Verses is a human document. The eternal reality of Creation is blurred because truth of life is drowned into its superficial fabrication. The distortion of fact by show-off artifices has stripped humans of true life and gratified living. The clueless humans do not know how to pull up a completeness of living before death strikes.

The anthology is an approximation of life and death as a guide to true love and living in a redolent and simple manner while disseminating colors of divine philosophy. The verses carry evocative human messages with powerful thoughts, emotions and feelings. The beautiful depiction of life and death as well as unique description of living and love has touched the grand height of logic and excellence.

The sonneted sermons of the book have been ingrained into the core of the verses and never sound didactic. Getting into a few of them is getting stuck to whole of them on account of their thematic expression and charm of versification. The poet has made a bold experiment with the English Sonnet form aesthetically and effectively and the book affirms to be soothing for the readers and get them experience significant facts of life, living, love and death.